# Spike and the Camping Trip

Maoliosa Kelly
Illustrated by Melissa Webb

Spike went camping.

He had lots of camping stuff.

He put up his tent.

Crash! Bang!

He got out his lunch.

Munch! Crunch!

He had a snooze.

ZZZzzzzzzz

Drip! Drop!
There was a hole in the tent!

Splish! Splash!
Spike got wet.

Crack! Crash!

There was a flash.

Hop! Skip!

He ran to his spaceship.

Zoom! Boom!
He was home soon.